12

Hidden
Heroes

BOOK TWO

More Bible people
who lived behind
the scenes

OT

DayOne

© Day One Publications 2011

First printed 2011

ISBN 978–1–84625–273-0

Scripture quotations based on the
HOLY BIBLE, NEW INTERNATIONAL VERSION, 1984.

Copyright © 1973, 1978, 1984 by International Bible Society.

Used by permission of Hodder & Stoughton Publishers,
A member of the Hodder Headline Group.
All rights reserved.

"NIV" is a registered trademark of
International Bible Society.
UK trademark number 1448790.

British Library Cataloguing in Publication Data available

Published by Day One Publications
Ryelands Road, Leominster, HR6 8NZ

TEL 01568 613 740 FAX 01568 611 473

email—sales@dayone.co.uk

UK web site—www.dayone.co.uk

USA web site—www.dayonebookstore.com

Designed by **documen**
Printed by Thomson Litho, East Kilbride

Dedication

For my parents-in-law, John and Elsie.
Thank you for your love and encouragement,
and also for all your suggestions!

Contents

Matchmaking!
The story of Eliezer

1

(This story is based on Genesis chapter 24 and 15:2. Although Genesis chapter 24 doesn't actually name Abraham's servant, we have good reason to believe that it was Eliezer.)

E liezer stood beside the well just outside the town of Paddan Aram. He was tired. It was evening, and the sun was slowly sinking in the sky, taking with it the draining heat of the day. Soon all the women of the town would appear to draw water, taking advantage of the coolness of the evening.

Eliezer turned his attention to his ten camels. Even they looked tired! They had carried their loads more than 500 miles and they needed a drink! Eliezer shrugged his shoulders. Camels drank such a lot and it was a huge task to get water for all of them. The men who drove the camels along also looked weary; they needed a rest. Eliezer told them not to draw any water yet but just to sit and relax for a while. He walked from camel to camel, gently patting each one in turn until they were all kneeling down. He could feel excitement rising in the pit of his stomach. This was the moment he had been waiting for ever since his master, Abraham, had asked him to make this journey.

At first Eliezer had been shocked by his master's request. He had been Abraham's closest servant for more than fifty years and had served him faithfully through all the ups and downs of life. However, this request was by far the most important thing that Abraham had ever asked him to do.

Eliezer lifted up his head to heaven and began to pray. 'Lord,' he said, 'you know that my master, Abraham, has asked me to come here, to the land he once lived in, to find a wife for his precious son, Isaac. Please show your never-ending love for Abraham by allowing this to happen today.'

Eliezer looked round. Some women were starting to appear, their water jugs balanced carefully on their shoulders. How would he know if one of them was God's choice for Isaac's wife?

'Lord,' he continued, 'you know that I am standing here. I'm going to ask one of the women if she will get me a drink. If she says, "Yes, and I will water your camels too!" then please let this be your choice for Isaac's wife!'

Even before Eliezer had finished praying he began to glance round for God's answer. There was a beautiful young woman heading towards him. She walked past him and filled up her water pot.

Eliezer's heart was pounding against his chest. Could this be the one? He ran over to her.

'Er ... um ... excuse me,' he stuttered. 'Please may I have a little water from your jug?' He waited.

'Of course you can, sir,' replied the woman. Quickly she lifted the jug off her shoulder and poured him a drink.

Eliezer saw her glance at the camels. She spoke again: 'I'll draw water for all your camels as well, if you would like me to,' she said.

Eliezer simply nodded. He couldn't think of anything to say!

The woman emptied the rest of her water into the camels' drinking trough. Then she went back and forth to the well, collecting water until the camels had had enough to drink. Eliezer watched her carefully, wondering if God really could have answered his prayer in such a remarkable way.

When the camels had finished drinking, Eliezer took some jewellery out of his bag and gave it to the woman.

'Thank you,' he said. 'And can I ask whose daughter you are? Do you think there is any chance we could stay at your home tonight?'

'We have plenty of room for you and the camels,' said the woman. 'My name is Rebekah. My father is called Bethuel, and my grandparents are Nahor and Milcah.'

Eliezer could hardly believe it! Immediately he knelt down on the ground and thanked God.

'Thank you, Lord!' he said gratefully. 'You have led me to the very people I was hoping to meet! These people are part of Abraham's family; Nahor is Abraham's brother! You have answered my prayer.'

Rebekah hurried home to tell her family what had happened. Straight away her brother, Laban, ran to the well and showed Eliezer and the camel-keepers the way to the family home. Laban brought food and straw for the camels and water to wash the men's tired and dirty feet. Then the announcement was made that a meal was ready. Eliezer was hungry, but he knew that he couldn't eat until he had explained the reason why he was there.

'Please,' he asked, 'I don't want to eat anything yet. I want to explain why I'm here. Then we will be able to eat in peace.'

'All right,' said Laban. 'Tell us before the food is served.'

As clearly and concisely as he could, Eliezer explained that over the years his master Abraham had become a tremendously wealthy man. Then, when he and his wife, Sarah, were very old, they had been blessed with a son, whom they named Isaac. Isaac was now forty years old and Abraham knew that he needed a wife! Abraham wanted Isaac to marry someone from his own family: someone who would follow his God and would keep to the traditions of his people. The problem was that Abraham lived 500 miles away from most of his family, and there was no way of sorting out a marriage at that distance! So Abraham had sent Eliezer to Paddan Aram in the hope that he could search for Abraham's family and, from among them, find a suitable wife for Isaac. Eliezer described his prayer at the well and how Rebekah had appeared even before he had finished praying, and how she had done exactly what Eliezer had prayed she would do!

Everyone listened in silence. As his speech came to an end, Eliezer looked pleadingly into the eyes of Rebekah's father and brother.

'So please,' he asked, 'will you allow Rebekah to return with me to become the wife of Isaac? Please tell me quickly!'

Both Bethuel and Laban nodded their heads in agreement.

'We agree,' they said. 'It seems that God has led you here to us, and we will allow Rebekah to go with you.'

As soon as the agreement had been made, Eliezer undid some of his luggage and brought out special gifts for Rebekah and the rest of her family. That night, he slept in peace; he had completed the task his friend and master had asked him to do. He knew Abraham would be very happy.

The next morning Eliezer, Rebekah and her servant girls mounted their camels and set off on their long journey. Eliezer felt full of joy. The family had asked if Rebekah could remain with them for another ten days, but it was Rebekah herself who had announced that she wanted to leave today. Eliezer knew that Rebekah believed this was God's amazing plan for her, and also that she was impatient to meet the man with whom she would spend the rest of her life!

After many days of travelling, Eliezer began to recognize the rugged landscape.

'We're almost there,' he said gently to Rebekah.

Rebekah smiled shyly. She felt both excited and nervous. Eliezer spoke well of her new husband; it seemed that he was kind and loving and would take good care of her. However, Rebekah knew that she was so far from home that there was little hope of her returning there for a long time. She was alone in a foreign land. She glanced round at her servant girls. At least they had travelled with her; at least they were familiar faces.

Rebekah gazed round at the surrounding hills. So this was to be her home. The sun was just beginning to set, and in the distance she could see a man walking in the fields.

'Who's that?' she asked Eliezer.

Eliezer smiled coyly. 'That's Isaac,' he answered softly.

Rebekah quickly pulled her veil over her face and slid down off her camel. Her legs were like jelly and she felt sick.

Isaac walked swiftly towards them and greeted Eliezer. Rebekah could see him looking nervously in her direction. She hoped he would be pleased with what he saw.

Eliezer explained everything that had happened during the past few weeks and then the whole story was repeated to Abraham and other members of the household. Everyone was amazed at God's immediate answer to Eliezer's prayer, and they were overjoyed to welcome Rebekah into the family.

Rebekah's worries about the way Isaac would feel about her didn't last long. He quickly fell in love with her, and soon they were married and began their life together!

Eventually, Isaac and Rebekah had twin sons called Esau and Jacob. Abraham, Isaac and Jacob are three of the most famous people in the Bible, but we know very little about Eliezer. He is one of the Bible's hidden heroes. He was simply a servant who obediently carried out his master's wishes. He didn't complain or argue, but he trusted God to help him complete his task. Eliezer is a great example to us. He didn't push himself forward, but was willing to stay in the background and allow God to use him where he was. The Bible talks a lot about how we should be like servants. This means that, even if we are clever or have more money than other people, we should not think of ourselves as more important than others. It also means that we should go out of our way to care for and help others, even if we don't feel like doing it! There must have been many times on his journey when Eliezer felt like giving up—travelling 500 miles on a camel would not have been very comfortable! In the same way, God wants us to never give up helping other people. After all, God never gives up helping us!

What do you think?

1. Read Genesis 15:2–3. Why might Eliezer have been jealous of Isaac and not have wanted to help?

2. Have a look at Genesis 24:67 to see how we know that Isaac and Rebekah loved each other.

3. In the New Testament, read Philippians 2:5–7. If Jesus was willing to become a servant, what does that mean for us?

Strong arms!
The story of Hur

2

(This story is based on Exodus 17:10–13;
24:14; 31:1–2; and 1 Chronicles 2:20.)

Hur stood at a distance, watching proudly as his grandson Bezalel eased his way through the crowds to take his place at the side of Moses. Time had passed so quickly! It seemed such a short time since Bezalel used to pull himself up onto his grandad's knee and ask to be told the same story over and over again. Now here he was, a grown man about to embark on a task of enormous importance. (See the next story to find out what that task was!) A smile spread across Hur's face. His body might be getting weaker, his hair might be thin and grey, but seeing his children and then his grandchildren follow in his footsteps made up for some of the disadvantages of growing old. This was Bezalel's moment, the moment that God had prepared him for.

Hur's thoughts slipped back over his own life. He had seen so many amazing things happen. He had been there when Moses finally led the Israelites out of Egypt. He had watched all night as God drove the water of the Red Sea back into two enormous walls. He had walked across the dry sea-bed, full of wonder at the greatness of the God he trusted.

He'd seen other things as well: things that most of the Israelites knew nothing about, things that would always stay in his memory. Moses had been his close friend for many years. Together, they had been through both good times and bad; times when there seemed little to hope for, and other times when they had both gasped in awe at the power of God.

Hur settled himself down on a rock. He was getting older, but the past few months had taught him that, even though his body was ageing, God still had jobs for him to do. Hur smiled when he thought of his favourite memory. A moment when God had used him in a great way, despite all his weaknesses and failings, despite the fact that he was growing old …

It was less than two months since the Israelites had left Egypt. They had seen God lead them through the Red Sea and provide for all their needs. They had been fed by birds in the evenings, and in the mornings delicious-tasting thin wafers called manna had appeared on the floor of the campsite. It was an amazing time, but some of the people living in the nearby towns weren't too happy. They had become worried that the Israelites were going to take over their land, and a group of them, called the Amalekites, decided to attack them.

The Amalekites gathered all their troops together and marched towards the valley of Rephidim, where the Israelites had set up camp. Moses knew it would be a tough battle if Israel were to defend itself. Only a few weeks before, the Israelites were slaves in Egypt; now they were expected to fight together as an army against the well-known Amalekite warriors! He called together Hur and his brother, Aaron, and a young man called Joshua.

'Joshua,' he commanded, 'tomorrow you will lead Israel out into battle. We are old men; you are young. Go into the camp and choose the men you want to fight with you. I will go with Hur and Aaron to the top of the mountain and ask God for victory. I will hold in the air my staff, with which God has performed so many miracles, so that everyone can see that victory will come from God and not from our own power.'

Joshua did what Moses asked him. The next morning, he led the Israelite army into the Rephidim valley. The land was dry and barren. Huge mountains rose on either side, casting eerie shadows along the brown earth as the sun began to rise higher in the sky. The Amalekite warriors stood facing them at the far end of the valley. They were a frightening enemy.

Joshua waited. Moses had set off early with Hur and Aaron. They were all getting older and the steep climb would take them longer to complete than it would have done in years gone by.

At last Joshua saw the three men arrive at the summit. Moses raised his arms high above his head, pointing to the heavens, making it clear to all those around that victory would come that day, not from the skill of the army, but from God. The battle began.

Moses was right: it seemed that the Israelites would have an easy victory! As Moses' arms grew tired, he dropped them to his sides while he continued to watch the Israelites storm ahead. But it was then that it happened! Without warning, the battle changed. Suddenly, the Amalekites seemed to gain extra strength. The Israelite soldiers began to fall to the ground. In horror, Moses again lifted his arms towards the heavens, and immediately the Israelites revived and moved in front. Soon it became clear that whenever Moses' arms were raised the Israelite army was winning the battle, but whenever he lowered his arms the Amalekites moved ahead. The problem was that Moses was becoming more and more tired. His arms were beginning to ache painfully, and despite his determination he was struggling desperately to keep them in the air.

It was then that Hur had an idea. Nearby was a huge stone. Hur ran over to it and, with Aaron's help, rolled the stone towards Moses.

'Quick! Sit on here!' Hur ordered. 'We'll stand at either side of you and hold your arms up for you!'

Hur and Aaron grabbed hold of Moses' arms and held them firmly in the air. At once, the Israelites again moved ahead in the battle.

All day Hur and Aaron remained at Moses' side. Even in the hottest part of the day, when the burning sun beat down upon them and they felt dizzy and faint, they did not move. At last the sun set and Joshua raised the cry of victory from the battleground. Only then did Hur gently lower his leader's arms. He had helped the Israelites win their first major battle since they had left Egypt!

Hur now glanced again towards his grandson standing proudly at Moses' side. He hoped that Bezalel wouldn't make the same mistakes that he had made in his life. A gentle smile spread across his face. He was glad that, in years to come, people would always remember his moment of great triumph, and hopefully Bezalel would be proud of his grandad.

We don't know what eventually happened to Hur. We don't actually know very much about his life! What we do know is that he was one of the Bible's hidden heroes. He was rarely in charge as a leader (and when he was, things went badly wrong!) but he was always there to help his friend

Moses. Hur didn't push himself forward into important positions but was willing to stay in the background, simply doing the job of supporting someone else. People often like to look important, but the story of Hur teaches us that those who are simply willing to help others behind the scenes often have the greatest effect on people's lives.

What do you think?

1. When Moses went up to Mount Sinai to meet with God he put two people in charge of the Israelites until he came back. Who were those people? See Exodus 24:14.

2. Have a look at 1 Chronicles 2:50–51. Which famous town was founded by another of Hur's grandsons?

3. Can you think of people you know who may not appear to be very important but actually do lots of things that help you or others? Why not look for ways to say thank you to them?

Practice
makes perfect!
The story of Bezalel

3

(This story is based on Exodus 31:1–5;
35:30–35; Exodus chapters 37–40; and
1 Chronicles 2:20.)

*B*ezalel took his place alongside the rest of his family among the huge crowd of Israelites that had gathered. His mind was full of so many thoughts. The last few days had been strange. He smiled for a moment and laughed to himself. In reality, it wasn't only the last few days; the past few months had been almost beyond belief! First there had been the terrible plagues that had happened in Egypt; they were followed by the announcement that the Israelites were free to leave Egypt after all those years of terrible slavery. Then there was the dramatic crossing of the Red Sea and the pillar of fire that had led the Israelites in the right direction through the night.

Bezalel had been brought up to believe in the power of the God of the Israelites; after all, his grandad Hur was a great friend of their leader, Moses. From an early age he had been taught that God had a great plan for the Israelites. More than that, Bezalel had been taught that God had a plan for his life, too: something that he had been born for, a task that only he could complete. Bezalel had often wondered if that could really be true. After all, he was simply a former slave who had received no praise and who was beaten if he didn't work hard enough or if he made a mistake. His father, Uri, had encouraged him to work hard and to take every opportunity to learn new things. Bezalel had done as his father had told him. He had learnt all sorts of skills in Egypt and had been recognized as a skilful craftsman. Bezalel had been glad to leave Egypt, but at the same time he found it rather sad that now there was nothing he could do with all the skills he had learnt, except mend a few tents and tent poles!

Recently, though, Bezalel had begun to feel that something exciting was going to happen. He felt as if God was especially close to him, and he wondered more and more what plan God had for his life.

The noise of the people lessened to a murmur as Moses took his place on the raised ground at the front of the crowd. Everyone gazed intently at the face of their leader. He had summoned them together to pass on a message, and each person was eager to find out what he had to say.

'Welcome to you all!' Moses announced, his voice heard clearly by all those present. 'I have called you here today to bring you great news! As you know, I have spent a great deal of time up Mount Sinai over the last few weeks. While I was there, God spoke to me and told me many things. Today I want to tell you about one thing in particular.'

He paused and looked round the crowd. He seemed to be wondering what their response to his words was going to be.

'God doesn't want to remain distant from us,' Moses continued. 'He wants to live among us and be close to us. For that to happen, he's told us to build a house for him, a place where his Spirit can dwell, a place where we can go to worship him.'

A gasp went up from the crowd. A few people began to cry softly. Bezalel knew these were not tears of sorrow, but tears of gratefulness and joy. The Israelites had let God down so many times. Only a few weeks before, when Moses was on Mount Sinai, they had completely turned their backs on God and built a golden idol to worship instead of him! Yet, despite their wrongdoings, God wanted to be closer to them than he had ever been before. Bezalel could hear the gentle mutterings of people speaking quietly in wonder at the love and forgiveness of God.

Moses waited for silence before continuing.

'God has told me that the place he would like us to build will be called the tabernacle,' he said. 'It will be made of the best-quality wood and trimmed with rich, ornate fabric. It will be decorated with gold, silver, bronze, special gems and valuable stones. God has ordered that a special box be made to stand in a special part of the tabernacle and that the stones on which the Ten Commandments are written should be placed in this box. This box will be called the "Ark of the Covenant". He has commanded that lampstands, tables, candlesticks, altars, wash basins and all sorts of other things be made to go inside the tabernacle. He has also commanded that special clothes be made that will be worn by the priests who will work in the tabernacle. The plan God has given me must be followed exactly. The plans are very detailed; the designs are complicated. Each item must be made with great care, just as God has ordered.'

The crowd was now completely silent, each person waiting with bated breath to see what Moses would say next.

'It is up to all of you,' Moses said solemnly. 'If we are to do what God asks we will need to supply all the materials needed to build the tabernacle. God doesn't want anyone to give who doesn't want to; he only wants gifts towards the tabernacle that come from willing and thankful hearts.'

Moses bowed his head and waited. Bezalel looked round at the crowd, wondering what their response would be.

He didn't have to wait long. One by one, person after person, family after family, the Israelites went back to their tents and then returned to lay their gifts in front of Moses. Bezalel joined them, but his mind felt as if it was somewhere else. He knew it was a silly thought but he couldn't force it out of his head … If only he could help with the building of the tabernacle! He had learnt so many skills in Egypt and lots of people had been impressed with his work. If only Moses would allow him to be part of this building project! He shrugged his shoulders and walked back to where Moses was waiting.

The pile in front of Moses was enormous! Some people had brought wood, others jewellery, still others precious metal objects. Some began to spin goats' hair to make the fabric for the priests' clothes and the tabernacle walls. The people's response was amazing. All of them were full of joy, thrilled that they could do something for the God who loved them so much.

As Bezalel joined the crowd, Moses lifted his head to speak again.

'Thank you,' he said, obviously pleased. 'We have all we need to do what God has asked us to do, but the plan God has given me is extremely detailed. We need someone who can be in charge of all this work.'

A buzz went round the crowd; people glanced from one to another, wondering who that person could be.

Bezalel waited. He hoped so much that it would be someone he knew, someone who would allow him to help in some small way.

Moses interrupted people's thoughts. 'God has told me who the person is that he wants to carry out this task,' he announced. 'God has given this man many gifts. In fact, this man is a master at every craft: engraving, carving, designing, embroidering and much more. Better than that, God has also given this man the ability to teach others how to use these skills.'

No one moved as everyone waited for Moses to name the man.

'Bezalel, the son of Uri, the grandson of Hur, please come forward!' Moses commanded in a loud voice.

Bezalel looked round, wondering for a moment why everyone seemed to be staring at him!

'Go on,' urged someone close by, giving him a push. 'Go forward!'

Suddenly, Bezalel realized what was happening. Moses had said *his* name. It was to be *him*! He was the man who would be in charge of the building of the tabernacle. *Him!*

As if in a dream, Bezalel walked to the front of the Israelites and took his place alongside Moses. He couldn't believe it! All those long years in Egypt working hour after hour, all those times when crafts had gone wrong and he had had to start all over again, trying and trying until eventually he had mastered a new skill ... but now he could see that it was all for a purpose. God had a plan for his life. It wasn't a plan he could ever have imagined, but it was a wonderful plan, and Bezalel knew he would do his absolute best to make the tabernacle a building that God would be pleased with.

Along with other trained workers, Bezalel built the tabernacle. It was a spectacular structure, and when it was finished Moses inspected it and found that it was built exactly according to God's instructions. But aside from his part in the building of the tabernacle, we know little about Bezalel. What we do know is that Bezalel is one of the Bible's hidden heroes. He was someone who was willing to allow God to use all his gifts and abilities in whatever way he wanted. This story reminds us that God has a plan for our lives, too. We all have different talents, and God wants us to use those gifts in the best way we can. No matter who you are, there are things that only you can do.

What do you think?

1. How do you think Bezalel must have felt when he stood at the front of the crowd after Moses had called out his name?

2. What happened when the work on the tabernacle was completed? Look at Exodus 40:34. How do you think Bezalel would have felt when this happened?

3. Have a look at Exodus 40:36–38 to see what else the tabernacle was used for.

The tiny army

The story of a soldier in Gideon's army

4

(This story is based on Judges 6:1–7:22. The Bible doesn't tell us the name of the man in this story, but we are going to call him Efran. Some of this story is exactly as the Bible tells it. Other parts are what the author imagines might have happened.)

*E*fran felt angry. He was sick and tired of spending day after day stuck in a hot, smelly, stuffy cave with hundreds of other people. It seemed as if they had been hiding here for weeks now, and if rumours were to be believed, it would be a long time before they could leave.

'I need to get out of here,' he muttered to himself. 'I don't want to waste my life hiding away in fear!'

The problem was that all the Israelites were in hiding: some in the mountains, some in caves, and others in all sorts of imaginative places where they thought the attacking Midianite army would never look!

Efran couldn't understand it. Ever since he was a small boy he had heard the great stories of how God had protected the Israelites in the past. He had been taught that God had performed amazing miracles to rescue them from slavery in Egypt and had brought them into a beautiful land that was a special place for them to live in. Now everyone was terrified! Armies from the surrounding countries kept raiding Israel. They had burnt their crops, taken all the sheep, goats, cattle and donkeys, and all the Israelites were in great danger of starvation.

Efran heard the muttering of an old man lying on a mat beside him. Somehow the mumbled prayer gave him hope. It was strange how, in the last few days, as people had become more and more desperate, the sound of prayer had become more common. It was as if people suddenly realized that they couldn't survive on their own; their only hope now was to trust in God. More and more people seemed to be starting to pray, and God had sent a message to them through one of the prophets, saying that he was very disappointed that the Israelites had starting worshipping the false gods called Baal and Asherah. Many people had said they were sorry for turning against the true God, but no one had yet mustered the courage to do anything about it. In the town, the altars set up to help the people worship these gods of wood and stone still stood there untouched, as if announcing to the world that the Israelites didn't truly want to follow their God.

A loud shout from outside halted Efran's thoughts. He immediately grabbed his sword and ran towards the cave's entrance. If this was an attack, he was ready to fight.

'Put your sword down, Efran,' ordered a man's voice. 'I'm not an attacking army! I've just brought some news.'

The people gathered round to listen; they liked a good story.

'You'll never believe it!' the man continued. 'I've come from the town. This morning there was uproar! In the night, someone had gone and destroyed the two altars to Baal and Asherah!'

Everyone gasped. A few older people cheered quietly. Whoever had destroyed them must be mad! This person would surely be killed!

'Who did it?' someone asked eagerly.

The messenger paused for greater effect.

'Gideon,' he announced. 'Gideon, the son of Joash.'

'Gideon?' gasped everyone at once. 'But he's nothing but a scared little boy!'

'Not any more,' corrected the messenger. 'Apparently, an angel appeared to him and announced that he was the one God was going to use to rescue the Israelites from all the invading armies! The angel called him a "mighty warrior"!'

A ripple of laughter spread through the listening group. Everyone knew that Gideon's family were weak, certainly not good fighters!

'Well,' continued the messenger. 'Apparently, Gideon tried to explain that he is the least important in his family and that his family is considered the weakest family around, but the angel took no notice! He performed a couple of miracles to prove what he said, and that was it! Last night, Gideon sneaked out of the house with some of the family's servants and together they destroyed the altars. This morning, loads of the townspeople were furious but Joash, Gideon's dad, stood up and announced that if Baal really had any strength at all, then surely he could stand up for himself! So everyone went home!'

Efran moved away from the crowd and sat down on a rock. Excitement was stirring in the pit of his stomach. Could this be it? Surely a visitation from an angel meant that God was on the move, didn't it?

It was a few days later that Efran's questions were answered. He was ready and waiting. Messages had been received announcing that a huge army, led by the Midianites, had gathered in the Valley at Jezreel to fight against Israel. This was nothing new, except that this time it seemed that the battle would be even shorter. The Israelites were so weak from lack of food that it was unlikely they could put up any sort of a fight.

A sound caused Efran to suddenly place his hand behind his ear. Surely that was it! The sound echoed across the desolate wasteland that surrounded his cave. It was the noise of a horn being blown loudly—the summons to war!

Without hesitation, Efran grabbed his sword. It had to be Gideon! At last, someone to lead them into battle! Crowds of young men appeared now, all of them running from caves and crevices, all heading towards the town to take their positions to fight for their land.

Efran arrived in town to find the place buzzing with excitement. Gideon had sent messages to all the surrounding towns and villages, calling the Israelites to meet together to fight. They had arrived in their thousands.

Gideon stood up and addressed the crowd. Efran was struck by the ordinariness of their leader. Was it really possible that this untrained young man could be successful against the huge armies that were awaiting them? He pushed the thought out of his mind. God had done amazing things in the past ... he could easily do them again!

Early the next morning, Gideon and his army marched out of the town towards the battlefield. There were 32,000 soldiers! When they were just a few miles from the valley in which the attacking army was gathered, Gideon allowed the men to stop for a rest. It was then that he made his surprising announcement.

Efran and the other Israelites were silent as Gideon stood before them.

'God has spoken to me,' he announced. 'He says that, if our army were too big and we were to win the battle, all of us would be tempted to boast that we beat our enemies by our own strength, not by the power of God. Therefore, God says that if any of you are frightened, you may leave this mountain on which we stand. You are free to go home. Go in peace.'

Efran looked round at the faces close beside him. Surely

none of them had come this far simply to turn around and run away! At first, no one moved, but then, slowly, one man after another turned and began to walk back the way he had come. Before long there were far more men leaving than there were staying to fight! It seemed that most were afraid; so many were certain that they would be defeated.

Efran remained where he was. He knew deep down that part of him was extremely frightened. He had heard so many terrible stories about the Midianite army. He didn't understand how the Israelites could ever win, and he didn't understand what God was doing by telling Gideon to send men home, but he knew that he wanted to be part of what was going to happen.

Gideon waited until all the movement had ceased. The army seemed small now; only 10,000 men had remained to fight.

'We will go down to the stream,' Gideon announced. 'We need to refresh ourselves before the battle.'

The men obeyed willingly. The water in the stream was clean and fresh, flowing from the well-known spring of Harod. Most of the men dived towards the stream; kneeling on the banks, they stuck their heads deep into the water to have a drink.

Looking round, Efran noticed that only a few men were drinking as he did. He had cupped his hands to collect the water so that he could lap it easily while keeping watch for any signs of the invading army. As they drank, Gideon motioned to those who were drinking from their hands like Efran.

'Those of you lapping the water from your hands,' he announced in a loud voice, 'please move over here. God has spoken to me again and he wants to use only you to win the battle over the Midianites. The rest of you can go home to your families!'

The men looked at Gideon in confusion. Had he gone completely mad?

Gideon saw their faces and repeated what he had said.

'Will those of you who are going home please leave behind any food and also the rams' horns that you use as trumpets, in case we need them,' he added.

Slowly, 9,700 men placed their provisions at Gideon's feet and walked away. The 300 men who remained stood in silence.

'We'll camp up on the hillside,' said Gideon. 'From there we can see the Midianite army in the valley below. I am sure God will tell us what to do next.'

As night-time fell, Efran gazed down into the valley. Campfires burned brightly in the Midianite camp. Efran had never seen such vast armies. From this distance, they looked like a swarm of locusts covering every bit of the ground in whichever direction he looked. He decided to try to get some sleep; at least that way he would be wide awake for the action!

Efran woke with a start.

'Get up!' a frantic voice was shouting at him.

Efran ran from his tent to join all the other bleary-eyed soldiers.

'Get up!' shouted Gideon again. 'God told me to go down to the Midianite camp, so I went down with my servant. We crept into the camp and overheard one of the men describing a dream he'd just had. One of the Midianites explained that the dream meant that we Israelites would definitely defeat them in the battle that we are about to have! All the Midianites are terrified!'

Efran could hardly believe what Gideon had said. How could a huge army be scared of 300 men?

'We must go immediately,' Gideon continued. 'We'll split into three groups and position ourselves on the hillside surrounding the valley. All of us will take a horn and a clay jar with a flame inside it. When I blow my horn, you must all blow yours and smash the clay jars so that the hillsides are ablaze with light. Then shout louder than you have ever shouted before, "For the Lord and for Gideon!"'

The men hurried to do what Gideon had commanded. Efran could feel excitement pulsing through every part of his body. This was it: the moment he had anticipated for so long!

Suddenly, the blast of Gideon's horn echoed across the valley. Immediately came the noise of the men's horns joining his. The sound was deafening. There was a moment's silence, then, without warning, light flared up on every side of the Midianite camp. People in the camp screamed in terror, and then the voices of the Israelite army filled the air: 'For the Lord and for Gideon!'

As the Israelites watched, the soldiers in the Midianite army began to fight one another in panic. Many were killed and many others ran away in fear.

From his position on the hillside, Efran watched in silent amazement. He hadn't even needed to raise his sword!

'Thank you, God,' he mumbled softly, realizing that he had seen things this day that would be remembered for ever. It seemed that God had heard their prayers and answered in a way far beyond anything they could even begin to imagine.

The Bible doesn't tell us the names of any of the men in Gideon's army, but each one of them was chosen by God to be part of an amazing victory. They are some of the Bible's hidden heroes. They acted with incredible bravery and trusted completely in God, even though it seemed totally impossible that 300 men could defeat the massive Midianite army. The men must have been scared, but that didn't stop them doing what they knew to be right. When we are young, there are times when we need to be brave and stand up for what we know to be right. It may be that we feel small and insignificant, but we should remember that God will always be with us and can use us in amazing ways.

What do you think?

1. Where was Gideon when the angel appeared to him? See Judges 6:11.

2. Have a look at Judges 6:15 to see how Gideon felt when the angel appeared to him. What did God promise Gideon in verse 16?

3. Read Ephesians 3:20. This verse sums up what Efran must have felt. Isn't it great that God is the same today as he was in the time of Gideon!

37

The accident!

The story of Mephibosheth's nurse

5

(This story is based on 2 Samuel 4:4; chapter 9; 17:27; and 1 Samuel 11:1–13. The Bible doesn't tell us the name of the nurse in this story, but we are going to call her Helah.)

Helah stood rooted to the spot. Her heart was pounding. She was terrified. From all over the palace the sound of panic filled the air. People were screaming, running wildly, grabbing belongings and shoving them into bags. Helah didn't know what to do. She looked round at the chaotic scene before her and tried to think clearly.

The news had spread rapidly through the palace since the messengers had arrived early that morning announcing, 'King Saul is dead!'

Not only had the great King of Israel been killed in battle, but also his son Jonathan had been killed. Everyone knew what that meant; it was normal practice in those days. If someone wanted to declare himself the new king, he would search out all of the dead king's family and followers and kill them! In that way, the new king could make sure that no one was in a strong enough position to challenge his right to be the king.

Helah could see the terror etched on each person's face. Everyone in the palace was either related to King Saul or had served in his royal courts as loyal followers. They were all in terrible danger.

Images of David ran through Helah's mind. She knew that the prophet Samuel had announced that David was God's choice as the future King of Israel. She knew too how jealous that had made King Saul. He had done everything in his power to get rid of David in the past; he had tried many times to kill him. Surely David would now get his revenge and rid the land of all Saul's relations and servants. She needed to escape, and escape fast!

Helah felt someone tugging frantically at her tunic. She looked down to see a small, tearful face looking up at her.

'What is it, Helah?' asked the young boy. 'Why is everyone crying?'

Helah gently stroked the little boy's head. She didn't know what to say. How did you tell a five-year-old such bad news?

'It's your dad,' she answered softly. 'Your dad and your grandad have both died. I'm really sorry, Mephibosheth.'

Mephibosheth gazed up at Helah. She had been his nurse for the past few years, taking care of him and looking after all his needs. He knew her better than anyone else in the palace. He snuggled up against her, tears running down his cheeks.

After a few minutes Mephibosheth raised his head, a puzzled expression on his face.

'But Helah, why is everyone looking so scared?' he asked. 'Why are they not just sad?'

'Well,' Helah explained simply. 'Everyone thinks that David will now become king, and unfortunately that means that we are all in great danger. David won't want any of your grandad's friends or followers to be around when he is king, so we all need to get away and hide from him.'

Mephibosheth looked confused. 'But Daddy always told me that David was his best friend,' he whispered earnestly. 'So surely David wouldn't hurt any of Daddy's family.'

'It's the way things happen, I'm afraid,' said Helah firmly. 'By tonight, we will all have disappeared.'

'But what about me?' Mephibosheth whispered.

Helah was silent for a moment. She could see from the frantic rushing about the palace that no one else had stopped to consider what would happen to this small boy. She knew that she needed to get away. It wouldn't be too difficult if she was on her own but, with a small boy in tow, it would be much harder to hide. How could she escape if Mephibosheth was with her? She had often taken him out for walks. He could manage for a short while but then he would moan and complain until they had turned round and headed back home. She would be better alone; there was more chance of survival.

Helah made a decision. 'Quick, Mephibosheth!' she ordered. 'We need to get your clothes.'

Together, Helah and Mephibosheth ran upstairs. Helah bundled some items of clothing and a few of Mephibosheth's favourite toys into a bag and then led the little boy into the kitchens. Already a lot of food had been taken but Helah grabbed what she could before taking Mephibosheth by the hand and leading him through a back entrance of the palace.

'Now, Mephibosheth,' she said firmly, 'we need to hurry as fast as we can possibly go.'

Mephibosheth nodded. He didn't really understand what was happening, but he was willing to do whatever Helah expected.

It wasn't long before Mephibosheth's small legs began to grow tired. He tried his best to keep up with Helah but he was growing weary, and all he wanted to do was go home.

Helah encouraged him to keep going but, before long, it was clear that Mephibosheth was making their journey dangerously slow. Helah could see that he was desperately tired, and she felt sorry for him.

'Come on,' she said gently. 'I'll carry you for a while.'

Gratefully, Mephibosheth climbed into Helah's arms and snuggled up against her. Helah struggled forwards.

She couldn't afford to stop. Any minute now, David's army might arrive. They must get as far away as possible. She was tired. Her arms ached painfully, but on she stumbled.

Then, without warning, *crash!*

Helah hadn't seen the stone in her pathway. She tried to protect Mephibosheth but she couldn't. Mephibosheth fell out of her arms and gave an agonized wail.

'Mephibosheth, Mephibosheth!' cried Helah. 'I'm so sorry! Are you OK?'

Mephibosheth lay motionless on the ground. 'I can't get up,' he mumbled. 'I can't feel my feet.'

Helah gazed at him in horror. Things were going from bad to worse!

'We need to keep going,' she said desperately. 'I'll have to carry you again.'

Helah walked on and on. Mephibosheth seemed to grow heavier and heavier. In the evening they sheltered in a cave for the night. Helah could see that there was something seriously wrong with Mephibosheth, but she comforted herself with the knowledge that at least they were both still alive.

The journey took Helah much longer than expected. She knew where she was heading but she hadn't expected to carry Mephibosheth all the way! She remembered that, many years earlier, King Saul had carried out an amazing rescue in an area of the country called Jabesh Gilead. The people who lived there had always been grateful; she felt certain that she could find someone in one of the surrounding villages who would be willing to protect Mephibosheth out of thankfulness to King Saul. At last, they arrived in a place called Lo Debar, at the house of a man called Makir. His home was certainly very different from the royal palace, but Makir welcomed Mephibosheth with open arms. Soon it became clear that Mephibosheth would be crippled for the rest of his life. Helah felt dreadful that the fall had injured him so badly but, despite that, she was happy that at least Mephibosheth was living. She had rescued him, and it seemed that Mephibosheth could now live the rest of his life in safety.

Mephibosheth lived in Makir's home for many years. He married and had a son called Mica. Many years after King Saul and Jonathan died, King David found out where Mephibosheth was living and sent for him. Mephibosheth was terrified, but King David promised not to harm him. In fact, not only did King David promise not to do Mephibosheth any harm, he actually invited Mephibosheth to live in the palace at Jerusalem with him! From then on, Mephibosheth even ate at King David's table, as if he were part of David's own family! David showed great love to Mephibosheth.

The Bible doesn't tell us anything else about the nurse in this story. What we do know is that she is one of the Bible's hidden heroes. She risked her own life to look after a small boy, even though she could simply have run away and left him. This nurse thought more about Mephibosheth's safety than about her own needs. It is often much easier to do what we want than to think about the needs of other people. It is easy to be selfish and always put ourselves first. The story of Mephibosheth's nurse teaches us that when we seek to help other people, things can still go wrong, but that is still the best path to take. Helah's actions were important enough to God for him to want them recorded in the Bible. They are a good example to us.

What do you think?

1. Mephibosheth had such a humble opinion of himself that he described himself in a strange way. Find out what he called himself in 2 Samuel 9:8.

2. In 1 Samuel 20:14–15 Jonathan, Mephibosheth's dad, asked David to do something for him if he should die. What was it? With this in mind, why do you think King David was so kind to Mephibosheth? Also see 2 Samuel 9:1. (You can read the story about David and Jonathan in *Hidden Heroes Old Testament Book 1.*)

3. In 1 Corinthians 13:4–7 it says, 'Love is patient, love is kind. It does not envy, it does not boast, it is not proud. It is not rude, it is not self-seeking, it is not easily angered, it keeps no record of wrongs. Love does not delight in evil but rejoices with the truth. It always protects, always trusts, always hopes, always perseveres.' How many of these qualities can you see in Mephibosheth's nurse and in King David? How many of these qualities can you see in your own life?

Never too old
The story of Barzillai

6

(This story is based on 2 Samuel 15:13–18;
16:14; 17:15–16, 22, 27–29; and 19:31–41.)

King David gazed sadly out of the palace window. How had it come to this? How could things have gone so wrong? He remembered the day his son Absalom had been born. He had been a lovely, happy baby who had brought so much joy to the palace in his early years. That seemed such a long time ago now. David had seen him only once in the past five years. Worse than that, David had heard that Absalom was, even now, trying to mass his own army so that he could attack Jerusalem, get rid of David and declare himself to be the King of Israel.

The pounding of running feet and the sound of shouting interrupted David's thoughts. A messenger burst through the doors.

'Your Majesty!' he shouted. 'It seems that Absalom has turned the whole of Israel against you! He's brought together a huge army. They are going to march to Jerusalem and crown Absalom as king!'

David jumped up immediately.

'Hurry!' he ordered. 'We mustn't waste any time! Gather all my family together. Tell them there's no time to pack anything that's not essential. We need to get away! If we escape before Absalom arrives, hopefully he won't attack the city and the people who live here will be safe as well.'

The king's messenger hurried to obey his orders and soon David's family, his bodyguards and all the soldiers who wanted to stay with David were ready to leave Jerusalem.

It was a sad procession that left the city. All the people, even King David, covered their heads and wept as they hurried along the road. It seemed likely that, if they ever returned, it would not be for a very long time.

The soldiers marched ahead of David's family, leading them north-east towards the Jordan River. It was a tiring and difficult journey, especially as they climbed wearily up the steep mountain slopes that blocked their path through to the Jordan. On and on they trudged, hardly daring to stop for anything other than to grab a few moments of sleep before they continued on their way. It was with great relief that eventually the people caught their first glimpses of the river Jordan glistening between the trees. At least here they could rest for a while before they waded through the water in the morning. As the people began to relax and unload the few possessions they had with them, David gazed sadly across the river. They had set up camp close to one of the Jordan fords, one of the few places where it was possible to cross the river without a boat.

A commotion behind him made David turn round. Two men were running towards him.

'King David,' they panted. 'We've come from Jerusalem. We've run as fast as we could. Absalom is going to set off from Jerusalem as soon as he can. Possibly even tonight! He is determined to kill you. You mustn't camp here or his army will have a greater chance of catching up with you. You've got to escape!'

Without hesitation, David ordered his soldiers and family to get ready to go. Wearily, they gathered their belongings and paddled out into the Jordan River. It was dark now, and the flickering lights of the torches danced on the water. The people shivered as the water level rose up their legs. The crying of tired children and the neighing of horses echoed eerily through the air. From his own horse, David could see the look of fear etched on each person's face. He lowered his head in despair. How had it come to this? There was a time when, wherever he went, the streets were filled with people cheering and chanting his name. Once he was the hero, the great King David, God's chosen king. Now he was fleeing in terror, dragging his family through the cold Jordan waters at midnight, all because of his unruly son. David had been through some tough times but this was definitely one of the worst.

The people reached the opposite side of the Jordan before dawn. Cold and shivering, they scrambled out of the water. There was no time to rest. On they marched, leaving behind the fertile plains of the Jordan, pressing on to where the land became a barren wilderness. Still they stumbled forwards, hoping that they could put as much distance as possible between themselves and the enemy. They were heading towards the city of Mahanaim, although no one was certain that they would be welcome there!

After many miles, Mahanaim came into view. A ripple of fear ran through the people. Would the residents of the city be pleased to see them, or would they be afraid of King David's arrival and fight against them in the hope of gaining some favour from Absalom? David waited. He knew that, if an army came out against him, there was no hope. Even the soldiers were weak from lack of food and sleep, his children could walk no further, and his family and servants looked ready to collapse. David felt like a failure. He wanted to give up. He had let everyone down.

As the Israelites watched, three men appeared at the city gate and began to walk slowly towards them.

The people held their breath and waited. Were they friends or enemies? One of them looked like an old man;

surely he hadn't come to fight. The men stopped in front of King David.

'I am Barzillai,' said the old man quietly. 'And these are Shobi and Makir. You must be so tired and hungry from your long march through the wilderness. We thought there might be a few things you needed.'

Even as he spoke, the clatter of horses' hooves broke through the silence. Barzillai pointed behind him towards the city gate. Horses and carts appeared, trotting across the rough ground, laden down with goods that the people could only distinguish as they drew nearer. A ripple of excitement ran from person to person.

'We knew that you had to pack quickly,' Barzillai continued, 'so we've brought sleeping mats, cooking pots, serving bowls, wheat, barley, honey, butter, cheese and lots of other things. We were sure you would need them and we wanted to help the family of the man we know is God's choice to be King of Israel.'

David's eyes filled with tears. He had felt so alone, so lonely. He had been close to giving up, thinking it would be better to run away with his family and hide for the rest of his life. Suddenly, though, he had realized that what he was doing was wrong. God had chosen him to be the king. He was a good king and he couldn't give up now.

'Thank you,' David whispered to Barzillai, taking the old man's hands in his own. 'I will never forget what you have done for me today. You had no need to do this and I will always be thankful.'

As quickly as they could, the Israelites prepared a meal. They ate ravenously. Suddenly, everything had changed. If there were people here in the city of Mahanaim who supported King David, then surely there must be other Israelites all over the country who would do the same. As soon as the meal was over, King David stood up.

'We will fight against Absalom!' he announced. 'We will trust in God to give us victory!'

King David ordered the soldiers to divide into three groups and appointed commanders over each section. His strength had returned; there was hope in his heart. Barzillai's kindness had changed everything!

In due course, the battle between the armies of King David and his son Absalom began. There was fierce fighting that spread out all over the countryside. Eventually, King David's army was victorious and, with great joy in his heart, he began to lead the procession of people back to Jerusalem. This time the journey didn't seem long and painful. The people sang as they went along, full of happiness that they could return to their home.

As David and his family approached the river Jordan to cross it on their homeward journey, a huge crowd of people came out to cheer them and help them. There was one person who stood out in the crowd. King David saw him and immediately climbed off his horse.

'My friend Barzillai!' David greeted him joyfully. 'Why don't you come to Jerusalem with us? I will take care of you there. You will have everything you need.'

Barzillai shook his head. 'Look at me,' he said, smiling. 'I am an old man—I'm eighty years old! I'm too old to come with you. I'm going deaf; I can't even taste my food properly any more. Just let me have the great honour of going across the river with you, and then I will go back home to my family, knowing that you are safe and heading to Jerusalem. But I have my son here. He is called Kimham. He would like to come with you. Will you take him and care for him?'

King David nodded.

'I will do anything you want,' he said softly. 'It is thanks to your kindness that I am still the king.'

With Barzillai walking proudly beside him, King David crossed over the river Jordan. Having said goodbye, Barzillai returned to his family, and David continued his journey back to Jerusalem.

The Bible doesn't tell us much about Barzillai; in fact, there are only a few verses about him. What we do know is that Barzillai is one of the Bible's hidden heroes. Even though he was a very old man, he went out of his way to do something so kind that it totally changed the situation David was in. The story of Barzillai teaches us the importance of thoughtfulness and the power that kindness has to change lives. It also shows us clearly that people are never too old to be used by God.

What do you think?

1. As King David got older, he arranged for another of his sons, Solomon, to become king after him. Before David died he spoke to Solomon and asked him to do certain things during his reign as King of Israel. Look at 1 Kings 2:7. Even though David was now very old, what had he always remembered?

2. Read Ephesians 4:32. How should we behave towards one another?

3. Look at 2 Samuel 19:35–36. Think about any elderly people you know. Remember that God counts them as vitally important. In fact, there are special things that only they can do.

The final meal

The story of the
widow of Zarephath

7

(This story is based on 1 Kings 17:8–24. The Bible doesn't tell us the name of the lady in this story, but we are going to call her Dinah.)

Dinah was worried. She hurried out of her tiny house and across the dry wasteland, her feet throwing up a choking cloud of dust with every step that she took. Her eyes searched the ground. She felt weak and helpless. She fought back her tears. It had been such a long time since there had been even one drop of rain on the land. All the crops had failed again and even the rich people were desperate for food. But Dinah was not rich. There had been a time when life had seemed good. Her husband had cared deeply for her and their young son, and the future had seemed bright. Then everything had changed! Her husband had died and she was left all alone to care for the child. As if that had not been bad enough to cope with, the severe drought of the past three years made it almost impossible to find anything to eat.

Dinah sighed heavily. Sometimes it felt as if no one cared. She lived here in the town of Zarephath, where widows were looked down on as people of no importance. Even when the land was producing plenty of food it was still a struggle for widows to survive. Deep down, she knew that she was one of the fortunate ones; at least she and her son were still alive!

Dinah went out of the town gates and began to gather sticks from the ground. Her stomach ached with hunger. She longed to eat a huge meal, but there was no hope of that ever happening again. In fact, she knew that her next meal would probably be her last. She swallowed as a lump formed in her throat. What would happen to them then? She thought of the tiny amount of flour and the few drops of cooking oil that were hidden safely at home. No one else knew where they were; she couldn't risk anyone stealing them. She would collect the sticks and then return home. She would build a fire and make a small loaf of bread and, once that had gone, she knew that they would die.

A man's voice interrupted her thoughts.

'Excuse me,' the voice said. 'Would it be possible for you to bring me a small cup of water?'

Dinah raised her head to see who was speaking. The man was a stranger and his accent made it clear that he was not from this area. However, he looked hot and tired, so Dinah nodded and began to walk towards the village well.

The man followed her at a distance, and when she had gone a short way he called to her again.

'And can you please bring me some bread as well? I'm really hungry!'

Dinah turned round to face the man. Didn't he realize what he was asking? Surely he knew that there was a famine! Surely he could see that she herself was starving!

'I'm sorry,' said Dinah, 'but I don't have a single piece of bread in the house. I have only a tiny amount of flour and a drop of oil hidden away. With these sticks that I have gathered I am about to make a final meal for myself and my young son. After that, we will die.'

The man looked directly into the lady's eyes and spoke gently.

'Don't be afraid,' he said. 'Go home and use the flour and oil to make a small loaf of bread for me. Then use the rest of the flour and oil to make bread for yourself and your son. The Lord God of Israel promises that the flour and the oil will never run out until the time when he sends rain back on the land and the crops begin to grow again.'

Dinah thought for a moment. What this man was asking her to do seemed like madness! What if he were wrong? What if he ate her bread and there was no flour or oil left? She would have given her last hope to a stranger!

However, there was something stirring inside Dinah. She had heard so many stories about the power of the God of Israel. She had heard that the reason there was a drought in the first place was because so many of the Israelites had turned their backs on their God and had started to worship an idol made of stone called Baal. Most of the people in Zarephath worshipped Baal, although many couldn't understand why the god of rain hadn't stepped in to help them.

Suddenly, Dinah made a decision. There was something in the way the man spoke, something in the stories she had heard. Maybe there was hope, even though what she was going to do appeared to be totally foolish.

'Come with me,' she said to the man.

Quickly Dinah led the way back to her home. She pulled the flour and oil from their hiding place and began to make the bread. Her small son watched her hungrily. She lit a fire and baked the bread. When it was ready, she handed it to the man. Dinah looked away from her son; she didn't want to see the disappointment in his eyes. Nervously, she walked back to where the flour pot and the oil jug stood on the table. She slowly picked them up and peeped inside. Her face glowed with wonder as she then lifted her head and looked at the man. He was watching her, but there was no look of surprise on his face. The pots were not empty! She knew that she had emptied their contents only moments before, but now there was more flour and more oil. As quickly as she could, she made some bread for herself and for her son to eat. Her heart was full of amazement. Suddenly, there was hope!

As they ate, the man explained that his name was Elijah. He was a special messenger from God, called a prophet, and he was hiding from King Ahab, who was searching everywhere to find him. King Ahab had been furious when Elijah had made his announcement that there would be a drought in the land for a few years unless the people turned back to following the true God of Israel. Elijah had been hiding near a stream for the past two years, and God had sent ravens to bring him food. When the stream had dried up, God had spoken to Elijah and told him to come here to Zarephath, where a widow would look after him!

Late into the night, Dinah sat listening to Elijah's stories about the amazing things that his God had done. Her small son lay sleeping in the corner. In the lamplight she could see his peaceful face. It had been such a long time since she had seen him sleep so peacefully. For months now, painful hunger pangs had woken him many times during the night. Tonight, though, he was not hungry.

As Dinah lay down to sleep, she peered up into the darkness. What a difference a day could make! And what a difference a living God could make to your life if you trusted him! For the first time in many months, she slept in peace.

Elijah stayed with Dinah and her son for a long time. Every day, they all had enough food to eat because, as God promised, the flour and oil never ran out. After some time, the son became ill and died, but God used Elijah to miraculously bring him back to life again. Eventually, God spoke to Elijah and told him to go and meet King Ahab. (See the next story about Obadiah.) After that, God sent rain on the land again and the drought was over.

The Bible doesn't tell us anything else about the widow and her son. However, we do know that the widow is one of the Bible's hidden heroes. She was very poor and had so little to give, but she willingly trusted God and gave away the little that she had. The widow of Zarephath is a great example to us of what it means to trust God, even when things seem to have gone wrong. She also shows us the importance of sharing and being kind to other people.

What do you think?

1. Have a look at Luke 21:1–4 to see how Jesus felt about another poor widow. (You can read about this story in *Hidden Heroes New Testament Book 1.*)

2. Galatians 5:22–23 talks about the 'fruit of the Spirit'. If we are following Jesus, this 'fruit' should be seen in our lives. Look at the list of nine qualities. How many of them can we see in the story of the widow of Zarephath? How many of these things can you see in your own life?

3. Read for yourself about how the widow's son was brought back to life in 1 Kings 17:17–24.

The secret caves
The story of Obadiah

8

*(This story is based on 1 Kings 17:1
and 18:1–16.)*

King Ahab paced anxiously backwards and forwards across the palace courtyard. The sun beat down from a cloudless sky. He was hot and sticky, and seething with anger.

'Elijah!' he hissed through gritted teeth. 'If I get my hands on Elijah, I'll … I'll …' King Ahab shook his head. Never in his wildest dreams could he imagine a punishment that was bad enough for Elijah!

King Ahab stood still for a moment and gazed up at the blue sky. He squinted in every direction, hoping that somewhere he would spot a cloud. He couldn't! For three years now, there hadn't been even one drop of rain in Israel. The whole of the land was brown and barren. Every stream had run dry and the crops had failed for another year. Famine was widespread, and both people and animals were in great danger of starvation.

'It's all *his* fault!' King Ahab fumed. 'Elijah, God's prophet! If only I could get my hands on him!'

The problem was that King Ahab could not get his hands on Elijah. In fact, ever since the day when Elijah had made the announcement that God would not allow it to rain for the next few years, the king had searched frantically for him, in every corner of every town. He had never been found, but King Ahab was determined never to give up searching!

King Ahab sighed heavily. He was angry, but he was also terribly worried. The drought was now so severe that even the royal household was short of water. His herdsmen had informed him that many of his animals had died and those that were still living were in a dreadful state. Ahab was desperate to save those that were left.

'It's no use,' he muttered to himself. 'If my servants can't find any water, then I'll do it myself.'

King Ahab thought for a moment. He needed help. He needed someone who knew the local area well; someone who knew all the tiny nooks and crannies, all the natural springs and oases.

'Obadiah!' he bellowed. 'I need Obadiah!'

The royal servants ran to Obadiah's office.

'Quick!' they shouted. 'The king needs you! He wants you immediately!'

Obadiah stood up and hurried to the courtyard. He was used to King Ahab's demanding ways. As the person in charge of the royal palace, he knew better than anyone that the king liked to get his own way. He also knew that when King Ahab was in a bad mood, he was totally ruthless and would stop at nothing to get what he wanted. For a moment, Obadiah wondered if the king had found out about his secret. He dismissed the thought quickly. If his secret had been discovered, an army of soldiers would have been sent immediately to get rid of him.

'Your Majesty,' said Obadiah, bowing to the ground. 'You sent for me.'

'Look at the sky,' ordered King Ahab. 'Not a cloud! My horses are dying. My mules are dying. And whose fault is it?'

Obadiah waited for the king to answer his own question.

'It's all Elijah's fault! When I find him, I'll … I'll … punish him more than anyone can ever imagine! When I find out who has been hiding him … that person will wish he or she had never been born!'

Obadiah remained still. He had often seen his master

like this and he knew that it was best to wait patiently for him to calm down.

'At least *you* are a loyal servant,' Ahab continued. 'At least I can trust *you*.'

Obadiah's face gave nothing away.

'You and I will go out and search the land. You sort it out. You will go in one direction, and I will go in the other. Surely between us we should be able to find some water! We'll check every spring and valley and see if we can find just a tiny bit of grass so that a few of my animals can survive. Who knows? We may even find Elijah!'

'I will arrange it,' promised Obadiah. 'I'll divide the land up and we will search everywhere.'

As Obadiah wandered back to his office to make plans, he quietly whispered his thanks to God. It was sometimes difficult to be a follower of God in the palace of a king who had turned his back on the one true God and was instead worshipping idols made of wood and stone. King Ahab was a weak man. Everyone knew that he did everything his evil wife, Jezebel, told him to do! She had said that the whole land should worship idols, and so that was the order that King Ahab had given. Most of the people of Israel had obeyed the king, although Obadiah knew for certain that not everybody had. Obadiah smiled to himself. It might be hard being a secret follower of God in the palace, but it was also extremely exciting!

Obadiah sat down and let his mind wander back over the past few years. He nodded in satisfaction. He well remembered King Ahab's fury when Elijah had made his announcement about the drought. However, he remembered even more clearly his own shock when Queen

Jezebel, in a fit of rage, had ordered that anyone who followed God must be killed. It had been at that moment that Obadiah realized why God had given him such an important job in the royal palace. He knew immediately that he was the only man in the whole country who could protect God's followers ...

It had been the middle of the night when Obadiah sneaked out of his apartment into the pitch-black street. He wore dark clothes and pressed his body firmly against the walls, keeping himself in the shadows. It was unlikely that anyone would be awake, but he was taking no chances. He hoped desperately that his message had been delivered safely ...
If not, he was in grave danger and his journey would be made in vain. Tiptoeing out of the city gates, he picked his way along the rough path that led into the remote, rocky wasteland lying high above the city. He had often explored here as a boy; he knew all the secret hiding places, all the paths that seemed like dead-ends but actually led to new unexplored territory! Obadiah speeded up; he must be there on time!

'Obadiah?' A faint whisper cut through the silent night. 'Obadiah, is that you?'

Obadiah's heart beat more quickly. This was it! Either his rescue plan was about to begin—or he had been found out.

'Yes,' he whispered back. 'It's me.'

In the moonlight, a man came slowly towards him and hugged him.

'We're over here,' he said softly. 'We found a small cave. We won't be safe here for long. Jezebel will send soldiers to find us soon and this place is easy to spot.'

'Don't worry,' Obadiah replied. 'I know just the place. King Ahab and Jezebel will never find you!'

The man led Obadiah to the cave entrance. Obadiah stooped down to go inside. A tiny light flickered in the far corner, sending eerie shadows dancing on the grey stone walls and the faces of the men hiding there.

'There are a hundred of us,' said the man in a low voice. 'I hope you've got a place big enough for us!'

Obadiah nodded and motioned to the men to follow him.

It was a long and lonely trek across the desolate rocky wilderness. The men walked in silence, glad that the moon provided a dim glow so that they could make out the silhouette of Obadiah ahead of them. Obadiah moved quickly. He knew that he must be back by dawn if he wasn't to raise the king's suspicions. At last, he paused. They were a long way from the city now, in an area so remote that it seemed unlikely that anyone had ever set foot here before. Obadiah pointed to a rock face.

'Our journey ends here, my friends,' he whispered. He bent down and moved a small pile of stones to reveal a tiny entrance just large enough for a man to squeeze through. He squirmed his way through the hole and disappeared. One by one, the hundred men followed him.

Quickly Obadiah lit a flame and the men found themselves squashed in a large cave. Obadiah hurried to the back of the cave and moved another stone.

'There's another cave behind this one,' he announced. 'Half of you go through, the rest stay here. Then, if Jezebel's army do find you, they will get half of you but they will never think of looking any further.'

With the men settled, Obadiah hurried back to the palace. He had promised to visit the men often, taking food and anything they might need. He was certain the hundred men would be totally safe in the secret caves. Now he must continue to run the palace without giving his secret away ...

Obadiah shook his head to remove all these memories from his mind. He needed to be quick. He grabbed his maps of the area and ran back to King Ahab.

'You set off that way, over the flatter ground,' Obadiah suggested. 'And I'll head towards the mountains. You are the king you shouldn't have to wander through such rough territory.'

'Thank you,' said King Ahab. 'I can always trust you, Obadiah, to look after your king.'

Obadiah smiled as he headed towards the mountain caves to begin his search. He had made sure that the king would never discover the secret caves; how could he, now that he was searching in the opposite direction? For now, the hiding place would be safe to be used by anyone else who needed to shelter there. Yet again, Obadiah was reminded that God had placed him in the palace for a very special and important reason.

As Obadiah walked along, looking for water, he looked up and saw the prophet Elijah coming towards him. Elijah asked Obadiah to go and bring King Ahab to him, and Obadiah did so. After that, there followed an exciting few days in the land of Israel. God carried out a great miracle through Elijah, and many of the Israelites stopped worshipping idols and turned back to the true God. After the miracle, God allowed rain to fall again on the land; the famine was over. For the time being, at least, King Ahab was happy and Obadiah returned to the palace and continued his royal duties.

There are only a few verses in the Bible about Obadiah. He is not well known. There is a book in the Old Testament called Obadiah, but this was written by a different man, not the one in this story. Although we don't know a lot about our Obadiah, we do know that he was one of the Bible's hidden heroes. He was in a position of great danger in the royal palace. If the king or queen had found out that he followed God, he would almost certainly have been killed. But this didn't stop Obadiah doing what he knew to be right. He used his position in the palace and his special knowledge of the land to help God's rescue plan happen. When we are young, it is good to remember that God has put us all in the places we are in for a special reason. God hasn't made a mistake! He has a job that only you can do for him. It may simply be helping someone or being a good friend—but God counts these things as vitally important.

What do you think?

1. Why don't you read 1 Kings 18:20–39 to find out about
    the great miracle that happened after King Ahab and
    Elijah had met.

2. Do you think that God sent just a little bit of rain or a
    lot? Have a look at 1 Kings 18:45 to find out.

3. There must have been many times when Obadiah felt
    frightened. Sometimes we too can feel scared. When we
    do, it's good to remember the special words that Jesus
    said just before he went back to heaven. Have a look at
    Matthew 28:20. Who is always with us?

Night-time rescue!
The story of Jehosheba

9

(This story is based on 2 Kings 11 and 12:1–2. The Bible doesn't tell us the name of the nurse in this story, but we are going to call her Adina.)

*J*ehosheba was gripped with fear. She could hear the commotion in the streets outside the windows. She could hear the screams and the crying. All she wanted to do was fasten down the shutters, cover her ears and close her eyes to block out every thought of what was happening. Instead, she wrapped her cloak firmly round her shoulders and pulled up the hood. She moved silently through the temple courtyard, glad that the flickering lamps allowed her to see the pathway, but afraid that they would provide enough light for someone to see where she was going. She dodged between pillars, keeping in the shadows.

Once in the streets, Jehosheba hurried as quickly as she could without drawing attention to herself. She headed towards the palace. The guards looked surprised to see her but allowed her to enter; after all, she was the daughter of King Jehoram.

Jehosheba glanced round nervously. No one was looking. As if her life depended on it, she sprinted through the servants' quarters, pausing for a moment to consider knocking on the door of the person she needed to find. But something stopped her. If she knocked, she would surely be heard and her plan would fail. And anyway, if the person she was looking for truly was as special as Jehosheba felt she was, there was no way she would be in bed at a time like this!

So Jehosheba hurried up the stairs towards the nursery. It was strangely quiet here. Silently, she lifted the door catch and sneaked inside. A hooded figure rushed towards her. Jehosheba jumped back in fright.

'It's me!' whispered the hooded lady. 'I didn't know what else to do.' She pulled back her cloak to reveal a tiny bundle.

Jehosheba lifted the corner of the blanket and bent forwards to kiss the tiny sleeping head.

'Thank you, Adina,' she whispered. 'I knew you would be with me, even if there was no one else in the world.'

Without a word, Jehosheba led the way back to the stairs. Even as they began to climb down they heard a door burst open on the corridor they had just left. Angry voices echoed off the stone walls. They moved more quickly.

'I'll take you the back way,' said Adina urgently. 'Not many people know about it apart from the servants. It will be far safer.'

Once out of the palace grounds the women paused to catch their breath.

'Where can we take him?' asked Adina. 'Queen Athaliah will search for him everywhere. There's nowhere that will be safe!'

'I know a place,' Jehosheba replied with certainty. 'Joash will be safe there. I checked it tonight before I came here. Follow me. If we get caught, I'll try to distract people while you go and find my husband. He's the only other person who knows about the plan.'

The streets were quieter as the women moved away from the palace, but they knew that would soon change. They dodged through the back streets of Jerusalem until the enormous walls of the temple towered above them.

'In here,' beckoned Jehosheba. 'Stay close and follow me. Don't say a word, and make sure Joash doesn't cry!'

Jehosheba led the way through the covered colonnades. The first glimmers of dawn were just beginning to appear and there was no time to lose. Jehosheba opened a small door that led down a dark, steep flight of stairs into a series of rooms that the temple priests sometimes used. She ushered Adina ahead of her and, having checked again that nobody was watching, she closed the door silently behind her.

'Go along the corridor to the farthest room,' ordered Jehosheba, lighting a torch. 'Get inside as quickly as you can.'

Adina obeyed, and soon the two women were safely bolted inside the small room. Only then did Adina lift Joash carefully out from beneath her cloak. She handed him to Jehosheba, who laid him gently across her knees and gazed at him.

'My tiny nephew,' she whispered softly, stroking his cheeks. 'What a lot of trouble you have caused us tonight!'

Joash began to stir and Jehosheba handed him quickly to Adina so that he could be fed.

'We need to keep him as quiet as possible,' she said, her face full of worry. 'His grandmother will be furious that he has gone missing. She will be determined to find him.'

'I couldn't believe it when I heard the news!' Adina said sadly. 'I still don't really understand what is going on. I just knew I needed to get Joash away from the palace as fast as I could.'

'You did a great job,' Jehosheba reassured her. 'What Queen Athaliah is doing is terrible. As soon as she heard that her son, King Ahaziah, had been killed, she seemed to go mad. Everyone has known for years that she is desperate to be in charge of the country, and she seems to have seized the moment to take power.

'But to kill all her grandsons?' Adina said with bewilderment. 'How could anyone do that?'

Jehosheba shrugged her shoulders. 'She is the daughter of Ahab and Jezebel,' she said firmly. 'And we all know how cruel they were.'

Adina looked down at Joash cradled in her arms.

'But she hasn't got you,' she whispered. 'And she never will,' she added, in a ferocious voice. 'We will stay here for as long as we need to. Your Auntie Jehosheba will bring us food, and we will bring you up to love God until the time is right for you to become king.'

'Your Uncle Jehoiada will help us,' Jehosheba added. 'He will know when the time is right.'

Adina bowed her head at the mention of the high priest. He was well respected in Israel, and Adina felt highly honoured to be part of a plan that involved him.

'I must go and see him now,' Jehosheba continued. 'He will want to know that everything has gone according to plan.'

She moved quickly towards the door and turned to look at Adina. 'Thank you,' she whispered, her voice full of emotion. 'I could never have done this without you.'

Adina shook her head. 'We did it together,' she corrected her. 'And we will protect him together until it is time for him to be king.'

For six years, Adina looked after Joash in the bedroom in the temple courts. Jehosheba secretly provided them with food and everything else they needed. At the end of six years, Uncle Jehoiada, the high priest, knew that the time was right to bring Joash out from hiding and declare that he was the true monarch of Judah instead of his wicked grandmother, Athaliah.

Joash became king at the age of seven! He was a good king who loved God and brought peace to the country.

The Bible doesn't tell us what happened to Joash's nurse or to Jehosheba. What we do know is that they are two of the Bible's hidden heroes. They did something extremely brave, and by doing so they allowed the family tree of David to continue as God had promised. Eventually, Jesus was born as a descendent of Joash.

Jehosheba and Joash's nurse were in exactly the right place at the time God needed them. They trusted God and put Joash's safety and protection above the value of their own lives. This story reminds us that God has put all of us in the places where we live, at this time in world history. God doesn't make mistakes! He has a plan for your life that only you, and nobody else, can complete.

What do you think?

1. How do you think Joash's nurse felt when he became king?

2. Look at 2 Kings 11:12, 19–20. How did the people feel when Joash became king? What was it like in the city?

3. Who helped Joash to be a good king despite the fact that he was so young? Find out in 2 Kings 12:2.

Only a child
The story of Josiah

10

*(This story is based on 2 Kings 22:1–23:30
and 2 Chronicles 34–35.)*

Josiah gripped the arms of his throne tightly as he gazed round at the faces lined up before him. His small legs dangled a long way from the ground, and the golden crown pressed down like a heavy weight on his head. He felt lonely. He had been told that his father was an evil man and a bad king, but that didn't mean that Josiah couldn't miss him, especially now that he was dead.

Josiah didn't really understand what had happened. Apparently, his father's officials had wanted to get rid of King Amon, and so they had assassinated him right here in the palace. Then, all the people in the land had been so angry with the palace officials that they had killed them. They had then brought Josiah into the throne room, lifted him onto the throne and crowned him the King of Judah. Josiah was glad that the people wanted him, but the problem was that he was only eight years old! He was so young and he had no idea how to be a king! He looked from face to face, wondering who could be trusted; he knew he would need so much help. The job he faced would not be easy, but deep down Josiah was determined to be a good king. He would do his best to follow the example of King David, the great King of Israel, the man about whom he had heard so many stories.

King Josiah was again seated in his throne room. He was now twenty years old. How quickly those twelve years had flown by! There had been so many things to learn, so many duties to perform. He smiled when he thought about that first day as king. He remembered the way he had swung his legs and wondered whether he would soon be allowed out to play. He had decided that day to be a good king and he had tried his best. So far, it seemed that he hadn't done a bad job, but he was about to take action that certainly wouldn't make everyone happy!

It had been four years since Josiah had realized that the stories about King David were more than simple tales about a brave soldier and king. The more Josiah had read them, the more he realized that David followed a living God who wanted his people to love him and follow him for ever. At the age of sixteen, Josiah knew that the most important thing in the world was to find out more about the true God and to find out what God wanted him to do with his life. As Josiah travelled around Judah, he became more and more worried. There was no evidence anywhere that anyone followed God. In every town and city there were idols built out of stone and wood that people would bow down to and worship. Josiah knew he had to do something about it.

The throne-room doors opened.

'Your Majesty,' a voice announced. 'All your officers are here as you commanded.'

Josiah beckoned them inside. He gazed round at the faces. Many of them would not be pleased.

'Having travelled throughout the land,' Josiah said in a loud voice, 'I have seen that the whole nation is full of idols and altars to gods that have no power. I want all these altars destroyed. I will lead you through all the towns and we will rid the nation of these false gods.'

There was silence in the court. Not everyone agreed with Josiah, but all of them would obey; after all, you never went against the word of the king!

It took a long time for Josiah and his officers to travel to every part of the land of Israel, but Josiah was determined to complete the task. In every town and village they destroyed anything they could find that had been used to worship other gods. Eventually, satisfied that Israel's journey back to following the true God had begun, Josiah and his men returned to Jerusalem.

Josiah sighed as he sat down on his throne. The past few months had been busy; it seemed that a king's work was never finished! Still, the temple was looking better than it had for years, and the workers were all so keen and happy in what they were doing. Josiah had now been king for eighteen years. When he had returned to Jerusalem after destroying all the altars to false gods, it hadn't taken him long to start work on his next project. For some time it had bothered him that the temple was in a terrible state. The Israelites had been so busy worshipping other gods that they had let the place that King Solomon had built for worship of the true God fall into ruin. The whole building needed renovating and all the rooms needed clearing out. So Josiah had got together a team of people to repair the temple. He had appointed a priest called Hilkiah to be in charge of the money for the project and, to Josiah's delight, people had come from all over Israel to give extra money to help with the renovation. Hilkiah had hired skilled craftsmen to work on the different areas of the temple; he even had musicians playing while the work was going on!

Suddenly, Josiah's peace was shattered.

'Shaphan, the secretary, is here to see you, sir,' announced a servant.

Josiah waved the man forwards. Shaphan bowed to the floor.

'Everything is going well at the temple,' Shaphan confirmed. 'But Hilkiah, the high priest, has asked me to give you this.' He held out a scroll.

Josiah unrolled the scroll and began to read. As he read, Josiah began to feel worse and worse. No wonder God was not pleased with the people! The scroll recorded the words of Moses and explained how God had rescued the Israelites from Egypt but, because the people turned away from him, God had allowed them to wander in the Sinai desert for forty years. It described ten special commandments that God had given to the people to help them live good and happy lives, and it gave the people all sorts of laws and guidelines as to the way they should live.

Josiah shook his head. The people had let God down so badly. However, there was still hope. Towards the end of the scroll it talked about how much God wanted to welcome the Israelites back as his special people, if they would only turn away from their wrongdoing.

Immediately, Josiah ordered that people be summoned to Jerusalem from all over the land. They arrived in their thousands: rich and poor, old and young. Together they went to the temple and Josiah stood in front of the crowd. Carefully, Josiah unrolled the scroll and began to read. He read every word while the people listened. The words of Moses had not been read for a long time and many of those present had never heard them before. When he had finished, Josiah rolled the scroll back up. In front of all the people he promised God that from then on, he would always do what God wanted him to do. He promised to keep all the commands and follow all the laws given in the scroll, and to live in a way that would make God happy. When Josiah had made this promise, all the other Israelites did the same, promising to turn from worthless idols to the living God.

As soon as the promises had been made, Josiah announced that a huge festival called the Passover was to be celebrated. The Passover was a special ceremony to help the people remember how God had rescued them from slavery in Egypt. In the past, it had been celebrated each year, but for a long time now it had been forgotten in the same way that God had been forgotten. Now Josiah was determined that the wonderful things God had done would never be forgotten again! The celebration was enormous and continued for seven days; God's people had at last turned back to him!

Josiah died at the age of thirty-nine. He was the King of Judah for thirty-one years. Throughout his life he followed God and tried to do what was right. Josiah is one of the Bible's hidden heroes. Not many people have heard his story, but he had an enormous effect on the people in the land over which he was king. When he died, even the great prophet Jeremiah wrote special songs to be sung at his funeral! Those songs were sung in Israel for many years. When we are young, it is easy to think that there is little we can do for God. It is easy to think that we must wait until we get older. However, this story shows us how important it is to follow God while we are still young, as it will shape who we are as we grow up. It shows us that decisions we make when we are very young can make a big difference to our lives. It also shows us the importance of reading God's words to us in the Bible.

What do you think?

1.   Have a look at Ecclesiastes 12:1 to find some brilliant advice!

2.   Jeremiah is one of the most famous prophets in the Bible. Have a look at how he felt about Josiah in Jeremiah 22:15–16.

3.   We know that Josiah was an amazing king. Have a look at the description of him in 2 Kings 23:25. How did he follow God?

A long way from home

The story of Meshach

11

(This story is based on Daniel chapter 1; 3:19–30; and Jeremiah 29:1–14.)

Hello, my name is Mishael, but most people call me Meshach. I live here in Babylon now, although my home is over 400 miles away in a place called Jerusalem. I often long to be back there, but I guess things will be very different from when I left. At least some of my family were brought here with me, although I don't know if the rest of them survived; I have no idea if my home was destroyed. What I do know is that King Nebuchadnezzar invaded my country with the Babylonian army and carried many of us off to this city.

I was born into a rich family. As a child I had many privileges, a lovely home, beautiful clothes and a good education. Life seemed good, until the news arrived that the Babylonians were on their way. We had been warned! Two of the famous prophets, Jeremiah and Isaiah, had told us that God would allow many of our people to be taken into captivity because we had constantly gone against what he wanted us to do. The journey from Jerusalem to Babylon was difficult. It was such a long way and we had with us many women and children. We would have been silly to try to escape. The Babylonians kept a careful watch on us and those who tried to get away were chained together to prevent them from attempting it again!

When we arrived here, we were given areas of land to live in. At first, lots of us believed that after a short while we would return to Jerusalem but, as the days passed by, we realized the truth: this foreign country was to be our home, probably for the rest of our lives. It was hard to imagine that we would never return home, but when a letter arrived from Jeremiah the prophet, we knew we had to get used to it. Jeremiah told us that God wanted us to plan to stay where we were. He wanted us to build homes, plant gardens, marry and have children! He also wanted us to try to live at peace with those around us. I especially remember one thing it said in the letter:

'I know the plans I have for you,' says the LORD. 'They are plans to help you and not to harm you. Plans to give you a future and a hope.'

Those words have stayed with me. It was so good to know that, no matter where we were and no matter what we had done, God was always there with us and we always had hope.

Anyway, not long after we arrived in Babylon, some of King Nebuchadnezzar's advisers came to see us. They wandered through our camp, talking to people and asking them questions before announcing that some of us were to go with them to live at the palace! It was certainly surprising news! Apparently, the king only wanted healthy, strong, good-looking men who had a brilliant education and would be able to pick up the Babylonian language quickly—not much to ask! Anyone chosen would spend three years in training at the palace learning all about the culture, history and traditions of Babylon. After that, the men would be given jobs in the palace, depending on how well they had performed.

I suppose I was quite flattered to be chosen, although I didn't want to leave my family. Three years was a long time, and I wasn't sure when I would see them again. However, the good news was that, along with many others, three of my friends were chosen as well! Before long I was on my way with Hananiah, Azariah and Daniel.

As soon as we arrived at the palace, the chief of the palace staff made an announcement.

'From now on,' he said, 'you will all answer to different names.'

He lined us up in front of him and read down a long piece of paper.

'Daniel, you will become Belteshazzar; Hananiah, you will be called Shadrach; Mishael, you will be known as Meshach; and Azariah, you will be called Abednego.'

We all knew what was going on. We had all been given names that were based on the names of Babylonian gods! It seemed that the king was determined that we would forget who we were and where we came from, and also forget the true God whom we followed.

Having found out where we were sleeping, all the new trainees were summoned to the dining hall for a meal. We were all so hungry after the busy day. As we sat down, our mouths were watering as delicious smells floated through the air from the kitchens.

Almost immediately, the servants appeared with huge plates piled high with food. Most of the men dived in hungrily. Only I, Hananiah, Azariah and Daniel waited. We looked from one to the other, all obviously having the same thought. As Jewish people it was against our laws to eat most of the meat set before us! It was Daniel who had the courage to speak first. He called over the chief of staff, who seemed to have taken a particular liking to Daniel.

'I'm really sorry,' Daniel said politely, 'but our religion means that we shouldn't eat this food. Would it be possible to eat something else?'

The chief of staff looked worried. 'These are orders from the king,' he stuttered. 'If you become weak and pale because you haven't eaten the best food, the king will have me killed!'

'Please just test us for ten days,' pleaded Daniel. 'During that time we will just eat vegetables. At the end of ten days, you can compare us with all these other men who are eating the king's food. Then make your decision as to what we must eat.'

Reluctantly, the chief of staff agreed. For ten days we all ate vegetables and drank water. At the end of the time there was no doubt at all: the four of us looked healthier than all the other men! It seemed that God was looking after us because of our willingness to do what he said.

After three years we completed our training and were presented to the king. After talking with us, he announced that out of all the men who had been trained, the four of us were by far the healthiest and the wisest! In fact, King Nebuchadnezzar was so impressed with us that he said that we were ten times better than any of the others! We were so pleased. To us, it just proved that if you follow God, you can totally trust him to take care of you.

Everything went fine for a while, until King Nebuchadnezzar had a bad dream and decided to kill us all because he didn't understand what it meant! Daniel managed to stop him and beg for a bit more time to work the meaning out. How the four of us prayed that night! And God answered our prayers, as he always does. Daniel explained to the king what the dream meant and then was promoted to be second-in-command in Babylon! Hananiah,

Azariah and I were the next in charge under him.

It was then that it happened! Suddenly and out of the blue!

King Nebuchadnezzar ordered skilled craftsmen to build an enormous statue out of gold. Nothing like it had ever been built before. It was ninety feet tall and nine feet wide! Then the king sent a message throughout the land, ordering that as soon as the people heard the sound of music they must bow down and worship the statue. Most people obeyed without question, but I knew that there was no way I could do that. I knew I followed the true God of heaven and I was not going to bow down and worship anything else, no matter what the consequences were. I was extremely pleased and relieved when I heard that Hananiah and Azariah agreed with me. All of us were determined that we would not do what the king commanded.

We should have known what would happen! There are lots of men who are jealous of Hananiah, Azariah, Daniel and me because we have been promoted above them. A few of these men got together and told King Nebuchadnezzar that we refused to bow down to him … and he was furious! He ordered us to be brought to him at once.

King Nebuchadnezzar did give us one last chance to worship him, but only after he had threatened us with being thrown into the furnace! We refused! We even boldly said that our God could save us from the fire; although we did point out that, even if he didn't, we would never bow down to any king anyway. That just made him even crosser!

So we were tied up by the strongest men in the army and King Nebuchadnezzar ordered that the furnace be made seven times hotter than normal! When the furnace doors were opened, the soldiers dragged us forward to throw us in. The flames were so hot that all of those soldiers who had pushed us in died because of the heat!

We fell into the roaring fire; we couldn't fight, we were tied too tightly. We lay there for a moment and then a strange feeling came over us. We were still alive! We struggled to sit up and look at one another. Our faces were full of amazement. All around us the fire raged on, but we were not affected by it in any way! Suddenly, we realized that our arms and legs were free! We stood up. Then we saw that we were not alone. Someone else was standing there with us! In complete wonder, we realized that God had sent an angel to us! We were going to be all right; God had come to the rescue. We walked around for a few minutes in the furnace, and then we heard King Nebuchadnezzar's voice bellowing from outside.

'Shadrach, Meshach, Abednego, servants of the Most High God! Come out!'

How our hearts sang! Not only were we safe, but now the King of Babylon had acknowledged that our God was real!

The furnace doors were opened, the angel left us and we walked out unharmed. King Nebuchadnezzar announced that there was no other god anywhere in the world that could rescue people in the way we had been rescued, and he gave an order that everyone in the land must worship our God!

So that's my story. I could tell you so many other amazing things that have been happening. Yes, we are far from home in a land that none of us wanted to be in, but we have seen first-hand the truth that God is with us wherever we are and whatever situation we find ourselves in.

We know little else about Meshach, Shadrach and Abednego, but what we do know is that they are three of the Bible's hidden heroes. They could so easily have fitted in with the practices of the land to which they had been taken. They could have opted for an easy life, bowing down to the king and enjoying the positions they were promoted into. However, they loved and trusted God and were determined to follow him, no matter what the consequences were. When we are young, there are times when we have to decide whether to stand up for what we know is right or whether to follow the crowd. It can be very difficult to do the right thing. This story reassures us that God is with us in every situation and that he has amazing power. It also shows us how important it is to have friends who follow God and who will stand with us when problems arise.

What do you think?

1. If you have ever been to a bonfire, you will know how quickly the smell of smoke gets into your clothes! Did Meshach, Shadrach and Abednego smell of smoke when they climbed out of the furnace? Look at Daniel 3:27 to find out!

2. God also rescued Daniel from a terrifying situation. You can read the story in Daniel 6:1–23.

3. Is God still able to do amazing things today? How does Hebrews 13:7 help us answer this question?

A sad day
The story of Baruch

12

*(This story is based on Jeremiah chapter 36;
32:11–13; 43:4–7; and chapter 45.)*

I t had been a long and difficult journey. Baruch's feet were cut and sore, but it was the way he felt on the inside that was hurting him most. He glanced sadly towards his friend Jeremiah. They had been through so much together. The past few years in Jerusalem had been hard to live through. All the neighbouring areas had been attacked and defeated one by one until eventually Jerusalem had been surrounded by enemies. It wasn't exactly unexpected! Jeremiah had announced years before that God was angry with the way the Israelites were living and that he would allow Jerusalem to be defeated if they did not turn away from the wrong things they were doing. But the Israelites had refused to take any notice and, although the prophet Jeremiah repeated God's message again and again, there were only a few people who listened; most just carried on with their lives as if God wasn't even there!

Jeremiah wearily lifted his eyes, meeting Baruch's gaze. Slowly he shook his head. There was nothing either of them could do but continue forwards with the army that had forced them to leave Jerusalem. They both knew that God had told all the Israelites not to run away to Egypt, and yet here they were, about to go back into the land that God had rescued them from all those years ago. It was a sad day.

Baruch looked down at the ground. He could clearly imagine Moses walking this same route but in the opposite direction, many years before. The people of Israel must have felt so differently then. Their hearts would have been full of joy that their God had rescued them from the cruel slavery of Egypt. Now Baruch could feel a lump in his throat; this was not as it should have been; this was not fair!

Baruch thought back over the years of his life with great sadness. There had been many ups and downs, but there was only one other time that he could remember when he had felt as bad as he did today. It must have been almost twenty years ago, and yet he remembered the pain and frustration as clearly as if it were happening now ...

It was during the reign of King Jehoiakim. Baruch had known Jeremiah for many years, but one day he had received a message asking him to go and meet him straight away. When he arrived, Jeremiah explained that God had told him to write down all the messages that God had given to him over the years. Each word was to be carefully recorded so that the Israelites could be reminded of everything that God had spoken. Baruch knew straight away why Jeremiah had called for him. From an early age, Baruch had been taught how to read and write. He had spent hours carefully practising his letter formation on scraps of papyrus and bits of leather, and now it seemed that God had a special use for him!

Day after day, week after week, month after month, Baruch sat in Jeremiah's simple room, writing down on a long scroll every word that the prophet dictated. He had to concentrate very hard; if he made a mistake writing down the words of God, he had to start all over again, until the scroll was absolutely perfect!

At last Baruch completed his task and it was time for the scroll to be read to the people. Usually, any important message would be read out in the temple. It was here that hundreds of people gathered day after day to worship God and to listen to the temple teachers speak about him. The problem was that no one liked the messages that Jeremiah kept bringing from God and so he had been banned from even going into the temple! Jeremiah called Baruch to him.

'Baruch,' he said, 'you know that *I* can't go into the temple, but *you* can! I need you to go and read out all the words you have written down. Maybe the people will listen to you and turn back to God.'

Baruch wasn't used to speaking in public. He was a writer, not a speaker! However, he knew that the people needed to hear what God was saying. In fear and trembling he made his way towards the temple. Once there, he stood up in front of all the people and read the words that were written on the scroll.

One of the men listening to Baruch's words was called Micaiah. As soon as Micaiah heard what was written on the scroll he rushed to the king's palace and told all the king's officials what Baruch had said. Immediately, the officials sent for Baruch and asked him to read the words out to them. As Baruch read Jeremiah's words, the officials became more and more worried. When he had finished, they turned to each other.

'We need to do something about this,' they said anxiously. 'We'll have to go and tell the king.'

Everyone agreed.

'Listen, Baruch,' they said. 'We have no idea what the king will say when he hears these words. You must hurry back to Jeremiah and go somewhere and hide with him. Don't tell anyone where you are going! Then, if the king is angry, he won't be able to do you any harm if he can't find you!'

Baruch sneaked away and the officials hurried into the

rooms of King Jehoiakim.

It was winter time, and the king was sitting near an open fire trying to keep warm. He immediately ordered that all Jeremiah's words be read aloud. A man called Jehudi began to read. He hadn't got very far when the king's voice rang out in the air.

'Stop reading and bring the scroll to me!'

Jehudi obeyed.

King Jehoiakim took the scroll and ordered that a knife be brought to him. Then he cut off the section of the scroll that had been read and threw it into the fire. The scroll burnt up immediately.

'Read some more!' ordered the king.

Jehudi obeyed.

After each section of Jeremiah's words had been read, the king cut off the words and burnt them in the fire. Soon nothing was left of the scroll but a pile of smoking ashes.

'Now go and find Jeremiah and Baruch!' the king ordered. 'Arrest them straight away!'

The palace officials rushed off, but they couldn't find the men anywhere!

Eventually, the news about King Jehoiakim burning the scroll reached Jeremiah and Baruch in their hiding place. Baruch was devastated. All his months of hard work had been for nothing. He had hoped so badly that the words on the scroll would make the Israelites turn back to God, but that hadn't happened. He had been looking forward to the future, but now he was hidden away in fear, with King Jehoiakim's army searching for him all over the country. The scroll, which was meant to record God's words for future generations of people to hear, was gone for ever …

Baruch sighed as he realized that the feelings he had now as he headed into Egypt were just the same as those he had felt then in his hiding place. The words he was now saying to God were almost the same too.

'Lord, it's not fair! I'm worn out with groaning! I can't get any rest. You don't seem to be here. You don't seem to care.'

Suddenly, Baruch lifted up his eyes to heaven. A sense of peace filled his mind. God had been with him then; God was with him now!

He remembered how, all those years ago, God had given Jeremiah a special message. A message not for anyone else, but a message just for him, Baruch.

'Baruch,' Jeremiah had said in the voice that he always used when he had a message from God, 'God says, "Baruch, you feel exhausted and full of pain and sorrow. You groan all day and don't have any rest. But I know, Baruch, and I will sort things out for you. Don't try to be great or important, because you matter to me. I will be with you wherever you go and I will save your life!"'

It was those words that had given him the strength to carry on. Those words had encouraged him to spend months re-writing the scroll, word for word.

It was those words that would encourage him now! It might be that everything seemed to have gone wrong, but God was still the same! God knew that he and Jeremiah wanted to do what was right. God knew that it wasn't their fault that they were being forced to return to Egypt.

Baruch turned to see Jeremiah watching him. A look of peace had spread across the old man's face, as if God was comforting him too. No matter what happened, God knew all about them. They would worship God together in Egypt. God was with them now, just as he had been in Jerusalem. If God was there, they had the strength to face whatever the future held.

We don't know what happened to Baruch when he arrived in Egypt. What we do know is that Baruch is one of the Bible's hidden heroes. He faced many difficult and discouraging situations, but he never gave up. It is very easy to give up when things don't go right for us. However, the story of Baruch teaches us that, when things go wrong, God hasn't left us on our own, but he wants to teach us something special through the hard experience. In the same way that God was with Baruch, God promises us that he is always with us, no matter what happens in our lives.

What do you think?

1. How do you think you would have felt if someone had torn up and burnt something that had taken you months to write?

2. Have a look at the book of Jeremiah in your Bible. You will see that the words that Baruch wrote down were saved for future generations to read!

3. Do you think it is wrong to sometimes feel sad and down in the dumps? Have a look at John 11:35 (the shortest verse in the Bible).

4. Read the last sentence in Matthew chapter 28. This was a promise that Jesus gave just before he went back into heaven. Why do you think this is such a special promise?

About Day One:

Day One's threefold commitment:

~ To be faithful to the Bible, God's inerrant, infallible Word;

~ To be relevant to our modern generation;

~ To be excellent in our publication standards.

I continue to be thankful for the publications of Day One. They are biblical; they have sound theology; and they are relative to the issues at hand. The material is condensed and manageable while, at the same time, being complete—a challenging balance to find. We are happy in our ministry to make use of these excellent publications.

JOHN MACARTHUR, PASTOR-TEACHER,
GRACE COMMUNITY CHURCH, CALIFORNIA

It is a great encouragement to see Day One making such excellent progress. Their publications are always biblical, accessible and attractively produced, with no compromise on quality. Long may their progress continue and increase!

JOHN BLANCHARD, AUTHOR, EVANGELIST AND APOLOGIST

Visit our website for more information and to request a free catalogue of our books.

In the UK: www.dayone.co.uk

In North America: www.dayonebookstore.com

Have you read the other Hidden Heroes books by Rebecca Parkinson?

Twelve Hidden Heroes – New Testament
978-1-84625-211-2, 96pp

Twelve Hidden Heroes – Old Testament
978-1-84625-210-5, 94pp

*Twelve Hidden Heroes – New Testament
(Book 2)*
978-1-84625-274-7, 103pp

Many of us dream of becoming rich and famous. We're fascinated by the people who seem important, but often we don't notice those who are working behind the scenes. The Old and New Testaments are full of mighty heroes who did amazing things, but there are also many 'hidden heroes'. These men, women, boys and girls were willing to stay unnoticed in the background, but their lives made a huge impact on those around them. In these books, Rebecca Parkinson tells their stories.

Rebecca Parkinson lives in Lancashire with her husband, Ted, and their two children. She became a Christian after realizing that the Bible isn't a boring old book, but a living book that is full of exciting stories that still change people's lives. A teacher and the leader of the youth work in her church, she now loves to pass the Bible stories on to others in a way that everyone can understand.

Have you read the Pocket Bible People books?

Pocket Bible People –
Ruth: More than a Love Story
Helen Clark
978-1-84625-078-1, 128pp

Never dismiss the book of Ruth as just a love story! It is the story of a woman who had to deal with the death of her husband and two sons. It is the story of a young bereaved wife who left her home, family and religion to follow the Lord and support her mother-in-law in her time of need.

Most of all, it is the story of a stronger divine power than you or I could ever imagine. It is the story of a God who loved Ruth and had a plan for her life. He led her through the hardest of times to a most wonderful conclusion.

Travel step by step through the book of Ruth, and find out for yourself how it is far more than just a love story!

Helen Clark was brought up in a Christian home in England and gave her life to the Lord at the age of sixteen. She has followed a career in nursing for fifteen years and in her spare time has been involved in youth work, helping to lead a group for young teenagers at her local church. She married Stuart in 2006 and they are currently living in Durban, South Africa.

Pocket Bible People –
Simon Peter: The Training Years
Helen Clark
978-1-84625-157-3, 112pp

What do you think of when you hear the name 'Simon Peter'? Perhaps you immediately remember how he denied three times that he knew Jesus—at the very time when Jesus was about to face the death penalty and needed his friends' support the most!

So what could we possibly learn from a man who failed like this? In this, the first of two books on Simon Peter's life, Helen Clark shows us that his story is one that should encourage us if we want to be followers of Jesus. We may find that we are more like Simon Peter than we thought, and that we make the same mistakes he made—but we can be transformed by following Jesus, just as he was.

Helen Clark was brought up in a Christian home in England and became a Christian at the age of sixteen. She has followed a career in nursing for over fifteen years and in her spare time has been involved in youth work. She got married in 2006 and now lives in Durban, South Africa, with her husband, Stuart.

Pocket Bible People –
Simon Peter: Challenging Times
Helen Clark
978-1-84625-158-0, 112pp

Simon Peter had been following Jesus for around two years by now, but he still had a lot to learn. He was still impulsive, and still prone to speaking or acting before thinking. What could Jesus possibly make of him?

This is the second of two books on Simon Peter's life by Helen Clark. As we follow his story, we see so much of ourselves in him—but we can also be encouraged by the remarkable transformation Jesus brought about in his life. How was he able to preach to thousands of people at Pentecost? Where did this once-cowardly fisherman find the courage to challenge crowds of Jews? Find the answer as you read on!

Helen Clark was brought up in a Christian home in England and became a Christian at the age of sixteen. She has followed a career in nursing for over fifteen years and in her spare time has been involved in youth work. She got married in 2006 and now lives in Durban, South Africa, with her husband, Stuart.

POCKET BIBLE PEOPLE –
Esther: God's Invisible Hand
Helen Clark
978-1-84625-204-4, 128pp

The book of Esther is hidden away and
not always well known. If you have heard
of Esther, perhaps you have thought of
her as a beautiful woman living an easy
life in a palace with a handsome, powerful
husband and surrounded by luxury. But if
you read her story, you soon realize how
wrong you are!

Esther's story actually involves
hatred, pride, ambition and violence,
and so has lots to teach us today. Here
Helen Clark describes the reality behind
the romance, and shows how God—the
hidden person in the story—helped Esther
to be courageous so that he could save his
people from destruction.

Helen Clark became a Christian at the
age of sixteen. She has followed a career
in nursing for over fifteen years and in
her spare time has been involved in youth
work. She got married in 2006 and now
lives in Durban, South Africa, with her
husband, Stuart.